POEMS FROM MY HEART

ISBN:9798320415796

DeLores May Richards

COPYRIGHT 2024

Contents

Contents 2
MT. ST. HELENS 3
LITTLE CHILDREN, DON'T YOU CRY 6
I REMEMBER IT ALL! 11
TIME DOESN'T CHANGE EVERYTHING 13
WHAT WOULD HAVE HAPPENED IF? 15
PRETEND 17
I ESCAPE 20
ODE TO RONNIE AUG 1, 2022 22
MY KINGDOM AT A GLANCE 24
THANKSGIVING 2022 26
MY HISTORY AND MYSTERY 29
REBECCA 32
IT WASN'T ALWAYS THERE 34

GOOD MORNING, LORD. 36
PIONEERS 38
BOOKS BY THIS AUTHOR 40

MT. ST. HELENS

It was back in 1980 when the mountain blew her top.
I couldn't change what seemed to be bizarre.
There were others watching who saw that same event

It was like watching a movie from afar.

And I stood there amazed that her life was so spent.

The mountain so tall was now laid low.
It was a big event that she would ever blow.

And another thing like that, I'd never know.

The ashes spread across the globe one Sunday morning
I stopped my car and watched the amazing sight.
She was 50 miles away, but she seemed so very near.
Her top had tumbled in across her side.

And over to the North, the ashes fell around.
She didn't seem to care just where they went.
They floated with the wind and then dropped onto the ground.
And covered all those cities in their ascent.

For many months, we felt her distress from the ashes that we saw.
They filled the gutters and the river wide.
They confounded all our cattle, and we spent money on our cars
to clean the ashes out of them from the inside.

Forty years have come and gone,
the trees are all renewed,
but the lake has vanished. I swam there as a child.

There are signs of life, but the pain I can't undo.
I cry as I remember that one day she went wild!

Chorus:

And the mountain blew her top, not something I could stop.
She sighed in pain as she went down ablaze.
She didn't want to stop, Her smoke was in the clouds,
And I could only stand there in a daze.

By DeLores May Richards 2022

LITTLE CHILDREN, DON'T YOU CRY

When I was just a little one, devoid of fears of life,
there came a most unusual event to cloud all of my sights.
For children who are only fit for play, worries are not there,
I found that I was not immune to the suffering we had to bear.

One day, my mother told us, "Come inside for a bit of a spell.
Let's sit and read and stay concealed, and to you both I will explain.
Some bad people want to take away our life."
She said this, and I was shocked. I was only five.

"Why, mother, would they want to take away our life?" I had watched a kitten die, so I knew.

"Why would anyone want to do that to someone else?" My little sister wiped away a tear, too.

"They want to take over everyone. They want to rule the world.

So, we must fight so we are free. It won't be an easy chore.

There are many things we can do at home to help with their defeat. First, of course, it is hard to bear—two of your uncles have joined the fleet."

"Oh, no, "I said. "Is it Uncle Don?"
Mother sat me down and said, "Yes, and Uncle Albert too.

They are both brave men.

They will protect us now, but we have a part to do."

"Little children, don't you cry." You know it will be better as time goes by.
God is with us, and we must comply.
With the duty we have been given, we will cry.
But we will not certainly die."

"How about Daddy? Does he have to go?" I lifted my foot in defiance and knocked over a chair.
"No, he will not. He has our family for which to care.
He's safe at home. But he does show concern and will be here for us all."

She proceeded to tell us what we must do.
"We must be careful with things and not waste.
And they will put a limit on the things we can buy.
It's the least we can do from this place."

"We have milk and butter and beef and a garden.
We won't starve or suffer a lot.
But we will have to be careful about the things that are bought.
So, remember what I told you and stay close to our house."

We discovered that the battles were not close at all.
But I remember the times we heard the sirens.
Mother turned out the lights, and she closed all the blinds.
A blackout we knew was again in place.

 At the movies, we discovered the scope of things as newsreels described the far-off war.

And the people who died and the many sad loads they bore.
We saw children dying in war-torn zones.
We saw children crying like never before.

And we said: "Little children, don't you cry!"

(World War 2   1939-1945) by DeLores May Richards

I REMEMBER IT ALL!

I remember the clam digging at Long Beach.
I remember fishing at Cold Creek.
I remember the times our dad took us
dipping in the Cowlitz River for Smelt.
Why do I remember?
Those things are so long gone.

And I also remember the fun times with relatives all over our yard, sitting and visiting, and the dinners we had and the friends we enjoyed. Do I want to go back? You can't go back in time!

I remember the house that my Dad built by hand. --one stick at a time, one little nail. And I remember the hammer that he used for it all. But you can't go back in time.

And the bathroom we finally got- one fixture at a time. I remember it all as my age passes on. And here I am at the end of the world. Who knows what time I will leave? But at least I will remember it all!

By DeLores May Richards

TIME DOESN'T CHANGE EVERYTHING

The physical things of life are gone.
The home I grew up in. The life I lived then.
My parents, my friends and all the rest.
They are leaving this life incredibly fast.

Do I miss my dog Gilmore? —He pulled me in a sled.
Do I miss the white kitten that I found dead?
Do I miss the neighborhood where I grew up? I miss them all without a doubt.
And sometimes I go back and dream of the things that once were there.
Then, I shed a tear, which shows that I care.
It's not easy, I admit, but they are no longer here!

But I look around me. I see the sun.
I see the moon. I note the sea.
These things were here long before me.
And so, I know that they will remain after I am gone from this earthly terrain.

I take my memories with me when I go to share with others I've met here below. Always with a thought and always with a dream as I'm lifted by angels- or so it will seem.

They will lift me higher than the sun, moon, and seas. They will set me in a place with a soft, gentle breeze.
They will provide a resting place where I will grow and bloom with grace.

Yes, I remember it all!   By DeLores May Richards

WHAT WOULD HAVE HAPPENED IF?

I've thought about this often as I research the deeds of God.
I may not have had you, mate of mine, if I had not followed where He was.
I think about it when I see you in the nearness of love true,
I think about it when I think about how close I was to not even meeting you.

That day was one of many. A Northwest girl- what was I doing here?
This desert was a wicked one—not one I could hold dear.
I answered the call to entertain in a band.
I wanted the fame that I could feel in my hand.

So, he came to the stage with another young man,
A fellow named 'Jimmy Wakely', the name of a star.
Except this young man had no guitar.

That is when I noted you and saw the winning smile with a pack of cigarettes on the arm of your white tee. Of course, it was the style.
With dark hair and a bashful look, you won my heart so fast.

I don't know how it happened when I look into my past.

We revealed where we would be the next day.

And, sure enough, you were there.
We got to talk a bit and laugh and sigh and care.
We knew each other's hearts right from the start, and from that day, I knew that we would never part.

So sentimental as it was, do you see God's plan?
I didn't at the time think it was because I joined a band!
I know now what I did not know then. I know now without a doubt that following God's direction is what it's all about!   DeLores May Richards

PRETEND

A little child is fascinated with the world of make-believe. It is something that they all like to see.

A world of fairies and Easter eggs and wonderous imitations of real cartoons and little elves and Cinderella and Snow white—
In little wonderlands, they dwell with things they think should be.

And we let them. We bring ideas for their play of things that do not exist.
We make them think that we believe that they are real.
Why do we do this? I do not know.
It's a part of their growing up.
Magic to their little lives. It has a certain appeal.

And when we see them slowly lose this play, we say, "Where did it go? The things she loved are tossed aside.

She's only eight, and yet we see a new view from her eyes.
And it doesn't matter —those Santas, bells, and whistles that she has seen.
She now is looking at reality, and it's something of a surprise.

But adults still enjoy a good 'Star Trek.'
They like scary movies.
So, you see, we retain a portion of the make-believe in our life.
We are not lost completely in this grown-up place of ours.
We go on, however, in a less magical fashion.
We know that the world remains in a bit of strife.

So, even we pretend. We do it all the time.
It's not a lie that we believe. It's a dream like a pie in the sky.
It's feathers and flowers and things nice and neat.
It's never the actual truth that we see.
A faucet that we can control.

It's a little bit of heaven, so we don't go down in defeat.

Pretend is a magic word. You want to be happy.
Pretend that you are. If you want to feel sorrow, pretend.
If you have a dream, pretend, pretend. It will come to you.
Is it any wonder that these things we can attend?
We think we believe, and we are.
It's a Belief in the magic of 'Pretend.'

I believe in it, don't you?

DeLores May Richards

I ESCAPE

When I am sad and I am blue and I just don't know what to do,

If things are not the way they should be and the way out I do not see,

When things get tough or the days are long and times are even rough, what do I do?
I escape.

There is a place where I can go where pain and stress I do not know.
It's a place where feathers float in the air, a place without any care,

A place of clouds and sky, a place
where no tears will fill my eyes.
I escape!

A place that has skies and breeze,
a place where I can see the trees.
The ocean slides along the shore; to
me, it beckons to the door.

I go backward in time again to things
I know, where I can see my rainbow.
Dreams are cheery for me now.
I escape!

    By DeLores May Richards

ODE TO RONNIE AUG 1, 2022

Well, I never thought it would happen.
James Howser turns 65.
The oldest of our eight has hit the beginning dive.
He didn't intend it to come so fast, and neither did we at our date, but he got there all the same.   But it's not an ending slate!

There's more to this life, you see. We see it every day,
And you can see it too when it gets in your way,
It's only a matter of minutes till all are in this land!
So please don't regret it. It's only an hourglass filled with sand!

The hourglasses make you appreciate the things you love and cherish.
You are blessed not to know the road ahead. It's fairish.

For it comes to all of us at some time in our lives—this thread.
It's not a simple matter. We can testify to what I've said.

For we've been there 27 years. We cannot understand it!
But there remains a well-traveled road, not one to only sit.
There are things to do and places to go. You can see them now.
Just look around you. Ronnie, and take a well-earned bow!

A road is for traveling. Don't stop and sit along the way.
It's meant to be a wonder—just remember to pause and pray,
And keep your feet traveling, there is so much left to do.
Your road will not end until you are completely through.

DMR

MY KINGDOM AT A GLANCE

Have you ever thought about the very fact that the Lord provided you with a kingdom here?

"What? I said. Yes! He provided a kingdom, but it is not mine to rule."

"If not yours, to whom does it belong?"

"It is His, of course."

"And how does He rule his kingdom?"

"I don't know! I don't! The world does not seem so good at all. Is He really guiding it?"

"Think now, another time—just one more time to sort the facts. Does a kingdom have subjects?"

"Yes, it does."

"And do the subjects obey the king?"

"Yes, they always do."

"And what does He say to do?"

"In Genesis, he says to rule the earth, the animals, the plants, all things living. But surely, that does not apply today. I don't know. Maybe it does. But aren't we different now?"

"There is one change—a simple change. Do you know what it is?"

"I'm not sure I can say."

"Another kingdom has come our way with Jesus. But it is the same. He says we rule the earth—but this one doesn't stop when we die. We will go on forever. His spiritual kingdom is composed of things we cannot see, things we cannot hear, and things that are not what they seem. Do you see it now? His subjects are all over the world doing his work. And that will continue forever, whether we live or die. Essentially, this kingdom is yours to rule. It is your kingdom at a glance.

"I see it now!" DMR

THANKSGIVING 2022

Here we are in another place, a place that is our own.

Thanksgiving dinner with all the fun of seeing all our kin.

And to let them all know, every one of them,

That they are where we have been.

We see the little ones growing up, who look a lot like us.

We see DNA in place, the chin, the eyes, big ears or not.

We wonder about these wondrous things.

Oh, what a glorious thing we have wrought.

This year, we have had three sick, or we would have had twenty-four.

These souls that came, we found so dear.

We met them all as we found them coming in the door.

And when they left, we cried a tear.

I don't think that we are so very different,

Then Great Grandfather's list of attendees.

No longer growing like we are,

He recited his loved one's list with ease.

The littlest on our list are noticed the most.

They all chase a dog and fall to the ground. We are glad that they all gather in the yard,

on this bright sunny day, mostly because of the sound.

Screaming kids are a welcome treat.

 For us oldsters in our rocking chair

But don't count us out; we won't miss a beat.

We tell them as much as their little hearts can bear.

So, Great Grandpa, remember, this all came from you.

So, we will share these things as we can.

While we are here, we'll share the load.

Of wondrous things in this kingdom of man!

So, 2024, go on your way, we'll look for another year again,

And maybe next time, new faces may come our way.

Anytime you come here, you're welcome like a friend,

There it is, and I don't know what else I can say!　　　　　DMR

MY HISTORY AND MYSTERY

It's not so much the history part that I enjoy so much.

It isn't the time that I spend on my writing.

It isn't the book sales I'm concerned about as such,

It's fun in the expression of things so exciting.

God gave me this life and said, "Do what you will.

I'm not about to correct your mistakes along the way."

He left it to me to travel the path and life fulfill.

And told me I would always certainly be okay.

By following where He would lead, I did.

Each step that I took was a wonderful road.

Made by God, nothing was forbidden.

But rewards in life depend on my choice mode.

So, I choose the right road each and every day.

And He gave me the rewards that I could see.

There is a choice in life, I have to say.

A road less traveled where few will be.

And now, at eighty-seven, I see it.

The fun that I've had on a less populated trail.

The things that I hold to my heart as most dear

These are things that I know will never fail.

So, I will write all the things that have meaning.

 From Great Grandfather will take a lesson or two.

He told his life in verse as long as he was breathing.

The end of his life was peaceful through and through.

So, I will keep on writing until that breath is done.

I'll write about the amazing world throughout history.

I hope that you will think of this too.

And solve, in your way, your life's mystery.

                DMR

REBECCA

Written in the 1980s (Rebecca died in a motorcycle accident)

If God isn't real, then there are no roses, no leaves in the spring, and no blooms on the tree.

If God isn't real, there is no Rebecca.

If God isn't real, there's no you and me!

Rebecca in motion like a big butterfly:

She touches us gently as she flits on by.

She gives us roses and a beautiful smile.

Now we give her flowers to remember her by.

She lives in our thoughts, and she lives in our hearts.

I see in my mind that she still flits through the room.

She's still with her God as she was on this earth.

I think of her when I see roses bloom.

If there is no God, then there are no roses.

No leaves in the spring, and no blooms on the tree.

If there is no God, then there's no Rebecca.

If there is no God, there's no you and me.

DMR

IT WASN'T ALWAYS THERE

I think I see a cloudless day, but it wasn't always there.

I think I see His face behind the sunshine in the air.

It wasn't always in my view, but now, at last, I see.

It was my first desire that there should be wisdom for me.

I dream of all the things that I have seen throughout my life.

The baby's smile, and much more, that I saw as a wife.

I can't forget my lover's touch throughout the many years.

When we shared hope through all and shared our many tears.

But it wasn't always there, and this I now know.

It came to me quietly amid the floating snow.

It came to me when others were rushing by.

It's nothing that demands a long, graceful sigh.

It's just there growing silently, not fast, not quick at all.

It's just the way He wants it, as we heed his loving call.

So, in the twilight of my life, this is the thing I want to share.

It is here now quite properly, but it wasn't always there!   DMR

GOOD MORNING, LORD

Most mornings, I wake up and speak to you first, Dear Lord,

I say, "Good morning, Lord, thank you for this glorious day!"

"Thank you, Lord, for all the blessings you are giving me each and every day,

Thank you for the birds, I hear singing, the ears I listen with, and thank you, Lord so much for the trees, and the eyes you gave me to see them. I think they are one of my favorite creations you made for us. Take care of my loved ones, and Lord, please be with those in need today; please bless them. Amen"

I then put on my slippers and go downstairs for some coffee. My Husband is usually reading the paper or watching TV, and we drink coffee and awake to the brand-new day.

This morn, my Husband and I awoke at 4:30. We both rose up and put on slippers and went down to make coffee together. It was far too early, but we were wide awake.

After a while, I felt a deep sense of sadness, I had not told you good morning. I tell you good morning every single day, every day, no matter where I am or what I am doing. I always awake and tell you good morning, Lord! My mood darkened, and I felt sadness and shame at my negligence.

From my cozy chair in the living room, I can see the sky brighten with the light of the day. I could see the white clouds billowing and lying low in the sky. It was supposed to be another rainy day.

But suddenly, red streaked across as if from a painter's brush, brilliant pink followed, filling the sky and changing to purple. Gold began next, with the rise of the sun, and painted a smile that only I could see. So brilliant was the sky that I raced to take a picture, but I could not record its beauty. The colors streaked across the sky in a brilliant but unexplainable sunrise on a cloudy day.

Lord, thank you for your beautiful "good morning" and for being the first to say it.

Diana Gulley

PIONEERS

History was made when pioneers moved west

Moved with their families, For homes of the best.

They fought off the Indians, the wolves, and the rains,

They fought in the valleys, the hills, and the plains.

They rolled over mountains, they moved through the streams,

They crossed the Columbia to fulfill all their dreams.

They went to find land, they went to find peace,

Homes for their families, to spread and increase.

No matter of terrors, they could not unveil,

For they found land ensuing, The dangers of the trail.

They surveyed the beauties. At the end of the trip,

And as we all know, it was worth every bit.

DeLores Nelson (Richards)
Sophomore 1951

BOOKS BY THIS AUTHOR

'Music from My Heart'

The author began her book-writing career at age 85. This first book includes her compositions from 1955 to 2020. It is especially directed toward her life stories and includes family pictures and history. The explanations and photos are done in color.

'My Great Grandfather's Poems Volumes 1, 2, 3, and 4.

Daniel Franklin Howard lived from 1841 to 1937. In his lifetime, he wrote poems about historical events. He served in the Civil War and was able to view many events firsthand. He published a historical novel called 'Oregon's first white men' in 1927. His desire was for one of his family members to publish his poems. The author includes letters and explanations. All volumes continue his beautiful work.

'Astoria Mysteries'

Book one is 'Gulley's Butcher Shop Clown.' (A murdered clown in the butcher shop.)

Book two is the' Sea Lion Scenario' (a beautiful young redhead found deceased among the Astoria sea lions.)

Book three: 'Uniontown' drugs and murder

Book Four: 'Missing' – Three young women disappear over two days, followed by a murder.

Follow history in Astoria, Oregon, with included photos of places to visit. Local restaurants are featured. The plot involves the Astoria Police Department and a fictional crime-fighting crew. The books also feature real live people from the city of Astoria. There, of course, is a romantic connection between tall Officer George Van and a suspect—Miss Mary Bell—a 5-foot musician. You might find yourself wondering who is real and who is not. You will enjoy the continuation of the story throughout the Astoria Mysteries series.

'Tenor guitar Program and songbook 2023 and 2024'

Made in the USA
Columbia, SC
15 May 2025

57898263R00024